plant-based
air fryer cookbook

TEXT COPYRIGHT © Alan Caplan

All rights reserved. No part of this guide may be reproduced in any form without permission in writing from the publisher except in the case of brief quotations embodied in critical articles or reviews.

LEGAL & DISCLAIMER

The information contained in this book and its contents is not designed to replace or take the place of any form of medical or professional advice; and is not meant to replace the need for independent medical, financial, legal, or other professional advice or services, as may be required. The content and information in this book has been provided for educational and entertainment purposes only.

The content and information contained in this book has been compiled from sources deemed reliable, and it is accurate to the best of the Author's knowledge, information, and belief. However, the Author cannot guarantee its accuracy and validity and cannot be held liable for any errors and/or omissions. Further, changes are periodically made to this book as and when needed. Where appropriate and/or necessary, you must consult a professional (including but not limited to your doctor, attorney, financial advisor, or such other professional advisor) before using any of the suggested remedies, techniques, or information in this book.

Upon using the contents and information contained in this book, you agree to hold harmless the Author from and against any damages, costs, and expenses, including any legal fees potentially resulting from the application of any of the information provided by this book. This disclaimer applies to any loss, damages or injury caused by the use and application, whether directly or indirectly, of any advice or information presented, whether for breach of contract, tort, negligence, personal injury, criminal intent, or under any other cause of action. You agree to accept all risks of using the information presented inside this book.

You agree that by continuing to read this book, where appropriate and/or necessary, you shall consult a professional (including but not limited to your doctor, attorney, or financial advisor or such other advisor as needed) before using any of the suggested remedies, techniques, or information in this book.

TABLE OF CONTENTS

DESCRIPTION 6

THE BASICS OF
A PLANT-BASED DIET 8

FOODS TO EAT AND AVOID 12

AIR FRYER: YOUR
KITCHEN COMPANION 14

BREAKFAST RECIPES 18

Vegan Tofu Scramble 20

Creamy Tofu Scramble 22

Mushroom And Avocado Fajitas 24

Oatmeal With Berries 26

Vegan Oat Pancakes 28

Apple Cinnamon Pancakes 30

Vegan Blueberry Oatmeal
Muffins 32

Air Fryer Avocado Toast 34

Apple Cinnamon Oatmeal 36

Vegan Breakfast Burritos 38

MAIN DISH 40

Lentil Patties 42

Tofu Stir-Fry With Vegetables 44

Cauliflower Fajitas 46

Quinoa Veggie Bites 48

Herb-Roasted Potato Wedges 50

Burritos With Guacamole 52

Vegan Chickpea Nuggets 54

Baked Eggplant With Tomato
Sauce 56

Veggie Tostadas With
Guacamole 58

Falafel With Hummus 60

Vegan Cauliflower Wings 62

Veggie Tacos 64

Vegetarian Pizza 66

Stuffed Grape Leaves 68

Veggie Sandwiches 70

Cauliflower Steak 72

Air Fryer Cabbage Steak 74

Green Beans And Potatoes 76

Air Fryer Sweet Potato And
Kale 78

Spiced Chickpeas 80

Air Fryer Young Carrots 82

Chickpea, Spinach, & Kale
Patties 84

Air Fryer Roasted Vegetables 86

Spicey Carrots 88

Roasted Artichoke Hearts 90

Red And Yellow Bell Peppers 92

Vegetarian Burrito 94

Brussels Sprouts With
Pomegranate Seeds 96

Sweet Chili Tofu Bites	98
Brussels Sprouts With Mushrooms	100

SNACKS & DESSERTS 102

Spicy Corn	104
Almond-Crusted Air Fryer Green Beans	106
Vegan Cauliflower	108
Spiced Air Fryer Nuts	110
Spiced Apple Wedges With Chia Pudding	112
Spicy Caramelized Bananas	114
Roasted Quince Stuffed With Nuts	116
Sweet Potato Chips	118
Carrot Chips	120
Beet Chips	122

CONCLUSION 124

DESCRIPTION

Discover the delicious world of plant-based eating with the power of an air fryer! The «Plant-Based Air Fryer Cookbook» is your ultimate guide to preparing healthy, tasty, and diverse dishes using one of the most innovative kitchen appliances.

This book is perfect for those who strive for a healthy lifestyle without sacrificing flavor and variety in their diet. Inside, you'll find:

- The Basics of a Plant-Based Diet: Learn which foods to include in your diet and which to avoid to feel healthy and energized.
- Principles of Using an Air Fryer: Master the art of cooking with minimal oil while preserving maximum nutrients and flavor.
- Variety of Recipes: From breakfasts to dinners, from light snacks to exquisite desserts – the book offers recipes for every taste and occasion.

The «Plant-Based Air Fryer Cookbook» is suitable for both beginners and experienced cooks who want to incorporate more plant-based meals into their diet. With detailed instructions and vibrant photos, you'll be able to easily and quickly prepare delicious and healthy dishes every day.

Join the plant-based revolution and enjoy healthy eating with the «Plant-Based Air Fryer Cookbook»!

THE BASICS OF
A PLANT-BASED DIET

A plant-based diet focuses on consuming foods derived from plants, including fruits, vegetables, whole grains, legumes, nuts, and seeds. The primary goal of this diet is to provide the body with all the essential nutrients while avoiding or minimizing the intake of animal products and processed foods.

Plant-based diets can vary in strictness, from vegetarianism, which excludes meat and fish, to veganism, which completely eliminates all animal products, including dairy, eggs, and honey. There are also intermediate forms, such as pescatarianism (excluding meat but allowing fish) and flexitarianism (primarily plant-based with occasional inclusion of animal products).

Principles of a Plant-Based Diet

Whole Foods: The foundation of the diet consists of whole, minimally processed foods. This means prioritizing fresh vegetables and fruits, whole grains, legumes, and nuts and seeds in their natural form.

Variety: Including a variety of foods in your diet helps ensure that you receive all the essential vitamins and minerals. Aim for a rainbow of colors and textures on your plate.

Avoiding Additives: Try to avoid foods with added sugars, salt, and artificial preservatives. The fewer additives in a product, the healthier it is for your body.

Moderation: Moderate food consumption helps maintain a healthy weight and overall well-being. Be mindful of portion sizes and avoid overeating.

Health Benefits of a Plant-Based Diet

A plant-based diet offers numerous health benefits. Here are some of them:

Reduced Risk of Cardiovascular Diseases: Studies show that people who follow a plant-based diet have lower levels of cholesterol and blood pressure, reducing the risk of cardiovascular diseases.

Diabetes Prevention: Consuming a high amount of fiber and low glycemic index foods helps maintain stable blood sugar levels and reduces the risk of developing type 2 diabetes.

Cancer Risk Reduction: Antioxidants and phytochemicals found in plant foods help protect cells from damage and reduce the risk of certain types of cancer.

Improved Digestion: The high fiber content in plant foods promotes healthy digestion and prevents issues such as constipation and diverticulitis.

FOODS TO EAT AND AVOID

The following foods are encouraged on a plant-based diet:

Fruits and Berries: All types of fresh and frozen fruits and berries.

Vegetables and Greens: A wide variety of fresh, frozen, and canned vegetables.

Grains: Whole grains like brown rice, quinoa, oats, and whole-grain bread.

Legumes: Lentils, chickpeas, beans, and peas.

Nuts and Seeds: Almonds, walnuts, chia seeds, flaxseeds, and sunflower seeds.

Plant Oils: In moderation, such as olive oil, flaxseed oil, and coconut oil.

The following foods should be avoided:

Meat and Animal Products: Beef, pork, poultry, fish, and seafood.

Dairy Products: Milk, cheese, yogurt, and butter.

Refined Sugars and Processed Foods: White sugar, candy, and baked goods made with white flour.

Trans Fats and Hydrogenated Oils: Margarine and products containing partially hydrogenated oils.

AIR FRYER: YOUR KITCHEN COMPANION

An air fryer is a modern kitchen appliance that uses hot air to cook food, creating a crispy texture similar to frying but with minimal oil or none at all. This method of cooking helps to reduce the fat content of dishes while retaining their flavor and texture.

Benefits of Using an Air Fryer

Healthier Cooking: By using little to no oil, air fryers significantly lower the fat content in your meals, making them a healthier choice compared to traditional frying methods.

Faster Cooking: Air fryers cook food quickly due to their high-speed air circulation, which can save you time in the kitchen. This efficiency allows you to prepare meals faster than conventional ovens or frying pans.

Versatility: Air fryers are incredibly versatile and can be used to prepare a wide variety of dishes. From crispy vegetables and healthy snacks to delicious baked goods, an air fryer can handle it all.

Convenience: With features like adjustable temperature settings and built-in timers, air fryers are user-friendly and make cooking more convenient. Many models come with preset functions for common dishes, simplifying the cooking process.

Easy Cleanup: Most air fryers have non-stick baskets or trays that are easy to clean. This feature helps to reduce the mess and effort involved in cleaning up after cooking.

Key Functions of an Air Fryer

Frying: Air fryers use hot air to cook food, creating a crispy exterior similar to traditional frying. This method requires only a small amount of oil or none at all.

Baking: You can use an air fryer to bake items such as muffins, cakes, and cookies. The hot air circulation ensures even baking and a golden-brown finish.

Grilling: An air fryer can mimic the effects of grilling by producing grill marks and a smoky flavor on vegetables and other foods.

Reheating: Air fryers are excellent for reheating leftovers, keeping them crispy and preventing them from becoming soggy.

Roasting: You can roast vegetables, nuts, and even small cuts of meat in an air fryer, achieving a perfectly roasted texture with minimal oil.

With its ability to create healthier versions of your favorite fried foods and its versatility in the kitchen, the air fryer is an invaluable tool for anyone looking to simplify and enhance their cooking experience.

BREAKFAST RECIPES

VEGAN TOFU SCRAMBLE

 Cooking Difficulty: 2/10

 Cooking Time: 15 minutes

 Servings: 2

INGREDIENTS

- 1/2 block firm tofu, crumbled
- 1/4 cup chopped bell pepper
- 1/4 cup chopped onion
- 1/4 cup chopped mushrooms
- 1/4 cup cherry tomatoes, halved
- 1/4 teaspoon turmeric
- 1/4 teaspoon smoked paprika
- salt and pepper to taste
- 1/4 cup chopped fresh parsley (optional)
- 2 slices whole-wheat toast
- avocado slices (optional)
- salsa or hot sauce (optional)

DESCRIPTION

STEP 1
Preheat your Air Fryer to 180°C (360°F).

STEP 2
In a bowl, combine the crumbled tofu, bell pepper, onion, mushrooms, cherry tomatoes, turmeric, smoked paprika, salt, and pepper. Toss to coat evenly. Spread mixture in Air Fryer basket. Cook 10-12 minutes, tossing halfway.

STEP 3
Serve on toast, with avocado, salsa, or hot sauce.

NUTRITIONAL INFORMATION

250 Calories, 10g Fat, 20g Carbs, 20g Protein

21

CREAMY TOFU SCRAMBLE

 Cooking Difficulty: 2/10　　 Cooking Time: 22 minutes　　 Servings: 2

INGREDIENTS

- 1 block soft or silken tofu
- 1/4 cup plant-based milk
- 1/4 cup chickpea flour
- 1/2 teaspoon turmeric
- salt and pepper to taste
- your favorite vegetables (e.g., spinach, mushrooms)

DESCRIPTION

STEP 1
Mash the tofu with a fork in a bowl. Whisk in the plant-based milk, chickpea flour, turmeric, salt, and pepper until smooth. Grease a baking dish or skillet.

STEP 2
Pour the tofu mixture into the prepared dish and spread evenly. Top with your choice of chopped vegetables.

STEP 3
Bake at 350°F (180°C) for 15-20 minutes, or until golden brown on top.

NUTRITIONAL INFORMATION

214 Calories, 10g Fat, 15g Carbs, 18g Protein

MUSHROOM AND AVOCADO FAJITAS

 Cooking Difficulty: 2/10 Cooking Time: 11 minutes Servings: 2

INGREDIENTS

- 7 oz mushrooms (sliced)
- 1 avocado, diced
- 2 tortilla
- 1 tbsp vegetable oil
- salt and pepper to taste

DESCRIPTION

STEP 1
Preheat Air Fryer to 400°F (200°C).

STEP 2
Slice mushrooms. Add mushrooms to Air Fryer and cook for 5 minutes, or until golden brown. Add avocado and cook for 1 more minute. Warm tortilla in a skillet or microwave.

STEP 3
Spread mushroom mixture onto tortilla, season with salt and pepper to taste. Roll up tortilla and cut in half.

NUTRITIONAL INFORMATION

256 Calories, 20g Fat, 30g Carbs, 10g Protein

OATMEAL WITH BERRIES

 Cooking Difficulty: 2/10

 Cooking Time: 20 minutes

 Servings: 2

INGREDIENTS

- 1/2 cup rolled oats
- 1 cup vegan milk
- 1/4 cup water
- 1/4 teaspoon salt
- 1/2 cup berries (fresh or frozen)
- 1/4 cup chopped nuts

DESCRIPTION

STEP 1
Preheat air fryer to 350 degrees F (175 degrees C).

STEP 2
In a medium bowl, combine oats, milk, water, and salt. Pour mixture into an air fryer-safe baking dish. Cook for 15-20 minutes, or until oats are thickened and heated through.

STEP 3
Stir in berries, and nuts.

NUTRITIONAL INFORMATION

300 Calories, 10g Fat, 45g Carbs, 10g Protein

VEGAN OAT PANCAKES

 Cooking Difficulty: 2/10

 Cooking Time: 25 minutes

 Servings: 2

INGREDIENTS

- 1 cup rolled oats
- 1 can coconut milk
- 1 tofu scramble (or 1/4 cup ground flaxseed mixed with 3 tablespoons water)
- 1 ripe banana, mashed
- 1 teaspoon vanilla extract
- 1/2 teaspoon baking powder
- pinch of salt
- fresh berries or fruit for serving
- maple syrup or agave nectar (to taste)

DESCRIPTION

STEP 1
Blend all ingredients together until smooth.

STEP 2
Preheat your Air Fryer to 350°F (180°C). Grease the Air Fryer basket with coconut oil. Pour batter into the Air Fryer in small portions, creating pancake shapes. Cook each pancake for 3-5 minutes per side, or until golden brown.

STEP 3
Serve with fresh berries, fruit, and maple syrup.

NUTRITIONAL INFORMATION

340 Calories, 17g Fat, 20g Carbs, 20g Protein

APPLE CINNAMON PANCAKES

 Cooking Difficulty: 3/10

 Cooking Time: 28 minutes

 Servings: 2

INGREDIENTS

- 1 cup all-purpose flour
- 1 teaspoon baking powder
- 1/2 teaspoon baking soda
- 1/2 teaspoon cinnamon
- 1/4 teaspoon nutmeg
- 1/4 teaspoon salt
- 1 cup plant-based milk
- 1/4 cup unsweetened applesauce
- 1 tablespoon maple syrup
- 1 apple, grated

DESCRIPTION

STEP 1
Preheat your Air Fryer to 350°F (175°C). In a large bowl, whisk together the flour, baking powder, baking soda, cinnamon, nutmeg, and salt. In a separate bowl, whisk together the plant-based milk, applesauce, and maple syrup. Gradually add the wet ingredients to the dry ingredients, stirring until just combined. Fold in the grated apple.

STEP 2
Spray the Air Fryer basket with cooking spray. Scoop the batter into the basket, creating small pancakes. Cook for 3-4 minutes per side, or until golden brown.

NUTRITIONAL INFORMATION

250 Calories, 7g Fat, 40g Carbs, 5g Protein

VEGAN BLUEBERRY OATMEAL MUFFINS

 Cooking Difficulty: 3/10	Cooking Time: 25 minutes	Servings: 2

NUTRITIONAL INFORMATION

150 Calories, 4g Fat, 25g Carbs, 3g Protein

INGREDIENTS

- 1 cup rolled oats
- 1/2 cup all-purpose flour
- 1/2 teaspoon baking powder
- 1/4 teaspoon baking soda
- 1/2 teaspoon cinnamon
- 1/4 teaspoon salt
- 1 ripe banana, mashed
- 1/2 cup plant-based milk
- 1/4 cup maple syrup
- 1/2 cup blueberries

DESCRIPTION

STEP 1
Preheat your Air Fryer to 350°F (175°C).

STEP 2
In a large bowl, whisk together the oats, flour, baking powder, baking soda, cinnamon, and salt.

STEP 3
In a separate bowl, mash the banana and whisk in the plant-based milk and maple syrup.

STEP 4
Gradually add the wet ingredients to the dry ingredients, stirring until just combined. Fold in the blueberries.

STEP 5
Spray the Air Fryer basket with cooking spray. Scoop the batter into the basket, filling each cup about 3/4 full. Cook for 8-10 minutes, or until a toothpick inserted into the center comes out clean.

STEP 6
Serve warm with additional maple syrup or a dollop of vegan yogurt.

AIR FRYER AVOCADO TOAST

 Cooking Difficulty: 1/10

 Cooking Time: 25 minutes

 Servings: 2

INGREDIENTS

- 2 slices of whole-grain bread
- 1/2 avocado
- juice of 1/2 lemon
- salt and pepper to taste
- optional toppings: red onion, cherry tomatoes, cucumber, seeds, cilantro

DESCRIPTION

STEP 1
Preheat your air fryer to 350°F (175°C). Place the bread slices in the basket and toast for 2-3 minutes per side, or until golden brown.

STEP 2
Cut the avocado in half, remove the pit, and scoop out the flesh. Mash with a fork and add lemon juice, salt, and pepper to taste. Spread the mashed avocado onto the toasted bread.

STEP 3
Top with your favorite toppings like thinly sliced red onion, halved cherry tomatoes, thin cucumber slices, seeds, or chopped cilantro.

NUTRITIONAL INFORMATION

140 Calories, 7g Fat, 6g Carbs, 5g Protein

APPLE CINNAMON OATMEAL

 Cooking Difficulty: 2/10 Cooking Time: 25 minutes Servings: 2

INGREDIENTS

- 1/2 cup rolled oats
- 1 apple, grated
- 1/2 cup vegan milk
- 1/4 teaspoon cinnamon
- pinch of nutmeg
- pinch of salt
- individual ramekins

DESCRIPTION

STEP 1
In each ramekin, mix together the oats, grated apple, milk, cinnamon, nutmeg, and salt.

STEP 2
Place the ramekins in the air fryer basket. Cook at 350°F (180°C) for 15-20 minutes, or until the oatmeal is cooked through.

STEP 3
Serve hot, topped with nuts, seeds, or berries, if desired.

NUTRITIONAL INFORMATION

250 Calories, 8g Fat, 25g Carbs, 8g Protein

VEGAN BREAKFAST BURRITOS

 Cooking Difficulty: 2/10 Cooking Time: 15 minutes Servings: 2

INGREDIENTS

- 1 red bell pepper
- 1 green onion
- 1 clove garlic
- 1/2 cup canned corn
- 1/2 cup canned black beans
- 1/4 cup chopped cilantro
- 1 tablespoon olive oil
- salt and pepper to taste
- whole wheat tortillas
- avocado for serving (optional)
- fresh lime juice for serving

DESCRIPTION

STEP 1
Preheat your air fryer to 400°F (200°C). Chop bell pepper and green onion into small pieces.

STEP 2
Toss vegetables with olive oil, salt, and pepper. Spread out in the air fryer basket and cook for 10-12 minutes, tossing halfway through. Add canned corn and black beans to the roasted vegetables. Toss to combine and cook for an additional 2-3 minutes. Fill each tortilla with the vegetable and bean mixture and top with cilantro.

STEP 3
Serve immediately with avocado slices and a squeeze of lime juice.

NUTRITIONAL INFORMATION

250 Calories, 10g Fat, 20g Carbs, 20g Protein

MAIN DISH

LENTIL PATTIES

 Cooking Difficulty: 2/10 | Cooking Time: 25 minutes | Servings: 2

INGREDIENTS

- 1 cup red lentils
- 1 onion
- 2 cloves garlic
- 1/2 cup breadcrumbs
- 1 tbsp flaxseed meal + 3 tbsp water
- 1 tbsp ground cumin
- salt, pepper to taste
- olive oil for greasing

DESCRIPTION

STEP 1
Cook lentils until tender. Finely chop onion and garlic. Combine lentils, onion, garlic, breadcrumbs, flaxseed mixture, cumin, salt, and pepper in a large bowl. Form into patties.

STEP 2
Grease air fryer basket with olive oil and cook patties at 400°F (200°C) for 15-20 minutes or until golden brown.

NUTRITIONAL INFORMATION

300 Calories, 8g Fat, 30g Carbs, 35g Protein

TOFU STIR-FRY WITH VEGETABLES

 Cooking Difficulty: 1/10 Cooking Time: 10 minutes Servings: 2

INGREDIENTS

- 1 block tofu
- 1 carrot
- 1 celery stalk
- 1/2 cup broccoli
- 2 tbsp soy sauce
- 1 tbsp honey (optional)
- 1 tsp sesame oil
- garlic, ginger to taste

DESCRIPTION

STEP 1
Cut tofu into cubes, vegetables into thin strips.

STEP 2
Stir-fry vegetables until tender. Add tofu, soy sauce, honey, sesame oil, garlic, and ginger. Cook for 5-7 minutes.

STEP 3
Serve over rice or noodles.

NUTRITIONAL INFORMATION

120 Calories, 8g Fat, 20g Carbs, 12g Protein

CAULIFLOWER FAJITAS

 Cooking Difficulty: 2/10

 Cooking Time: 22 minutes

 Servings: 2

INGREDIENTS

- 1 head of cauliflower, cut into small florets
- 1 red onion, chopped
- 1 green bell pepper, chopped
- 1/2 cup corn
- 1/4 cup fresh cilantro, chopped
- juice of 1 lime
- 2 tablespoons olive oil
- seasonings: salt, pepper, chili powder, paprika

DESCRIPTION

STEP 1
Combine cauliflower, onion, bell pepper, corn, cilantro, lime juice, olive oil, and seasonings in a bowl.

STEP 2
Spread the mixture in the air fryer basket. Cook at 400°F (200°C) for 15-20 minutes or until vegetables are tender and slightly browned.

STEP 3
Serve immediately with avocado slices and a squeeze of lime juice.

NUTRITIONAL INFORMATION

210 Calories, 7g Fat, 11g Carbs, 9g Protein

QUINOA VEGGIE BITES

 Cooking Difficulty: 2/10

 Cooking Time: 25 minutes

 Servings: 2

INGREDIENTS

- 1 cup cooked quinoa
- 1 cup grated carrot
- 1/2 cup chopped broccoli
- 1/4 cup chopped onion
- 1 egg
- 1/4 cup breadcrumbs
- seasonings: salt, pepper, garlic powder, paprika

DESCRIPTION

STEP 1
Combine all ingredients in a bowl. Form into balls.

STEP 2
Cook in the air fryer at 400°F (200°C) for 15-20 minutes or until golden brown.

NUTRITIONAL INFORMATION

275 Calories, 11g Fat, 25g Carbs, 17g Protein

49

HERB-ROASTED POTATO WEDGES

 Cooking Difficulty: 1/10   Cooking Time: 28 minutes   Servings: 2

INGREDIENTS

- 4 potatoes, cut into wedges
- 2 tablespoons olive oil
- 2 cloves garlic, minced
- 1 tablespoon dried thyme
- salt and pepper to taste

DESCRIPTION

STEP 1
Toss potato wedges with olive oil, garlic, thyme, salt, and pepper.

STEP 2
Spread wedges in the air fryer basket.

STEP 3
Cook at 400°F (200°C) for 20-25 minutes or until golden brown.

NUTRITIONAL INFORMATION

170 Calories, 4g Fat, 9g Carbs, 3g Protein

BURRITOS WITH GUACAMOLE

 Cooking Difficulty: 2/10   Cooking Time: 20 minutes   Servings: 2

INGREDIENTS

- 1 can (15 oz) black or kidney beans, drained and rinsed
- 1/2 onion, diced
- 1/2 bell pepper, diced
- 1 tomato, diced
- 1/4 cup corn
- 1 tbsp olive oil
- 1/2 tsp chili powder
- salt and pepper to taste
- 2 burrito tortillas
- 1/2 avocado, mashed
- 1 tbsp lime juice
- 1/4 cup chopped cilantro
- salt and pepper to taste

DESCRIPTION

STEP 1
Preheat Air Fryer to 400°F (200°C).

STEP 2
Dice onion, bell pepper, and tomato. In a bowl, combine beans, onion, bell pepper, tomato, corn, olive oil, chili powder, salt, and pepper. Place the mixture in the Air Fryer basket. Air fry for 10-15 minutes, or until vegetables are tender.

STEP 3
In a separate bowl, mash avocado with lime juice, cilantro, salt, and pepper. Spread bean mixture onto tortillas, top with guacamole. Roll up burritos.

NUTRITIONAL INFORMATION

250 Calories, 15g Fat, 15g Carbs, 5g Protein

VEGAN CHICKPEA NUGGETS

 Cooking Difficulty: 2/10
 Cooking Time: 27 minutes
 Servings: 2

INGREDIENTS

- 1 can chickpeas, rinsed and drained
- 1/4 cup breadcrumbs
- 1 tablespoon flaxseed meal with 3 tablespoons water
- 1 tablespoon mustard
- 1 teaspoon smoked paprika
- salt and pepper to taste

DESCRIPTION

STEP 1
Mash chickpeas with a fork. Add remaining ingredients and mix well.

STEP 2
Form into nugget shapes.

STEP 3
Cook in the air fryer at 400°F (200°C) for 15-20 minutes or until golden brown.

NUTRITIONAL INFORMATION

300 Calories, 10g Fat, 22g Carbs, 9g Protein

BAKED EGGPLANT WITH TOMATO SAUCE

 Cooking Difficulty: 3/10

 Cooking Time: 25 minutes

 Servings: 2

INGREDIENTS

- 2 eggplants, sliced
- 1 can crushed tomatoes
- 1 onion, finely chopped
- 2 cloves garlic, minced
- 1 teaspoon oregano
- salt and pepper to taste
- vegan mozzarella, for serving

DESCRIPTION

STEP 1
Air fry eggplant slices until golden brown.

STEP 2
Sauté onion and garlic in remaining oil. Add tomatoes, oregano, salt, and pepper. Simmer for 10 minutes. Layer eggplant slices in a baking dish, top with tomato sauce.

STEP 3
Sprinkle with vegan mozzarella and bake until cheese is melted.

NUTRITIONAL INFORMATION

180 Calories, 10g Fat, 5g Carbs, 7g Protein

VEGGIE TOSTADAS WITH GUACAMOLE

 Cooking Difficulty: 2/10	Cooking Time: 15 minutes	Servings: 2

NUTRITIONAL INFORMATION

Calories 300, Fat 10g, Carbs 27g, Protein 9g

INGREDIENTS

- 2 corn tortillas
- 1/2 red bell pepper, sliced into half rings
- 1/2 green bell pepper, sliced into half rings
- 1/2 red onion, sliced
- 1/2 teaspoon chili powder
- salt and pepper to taste
- 1 tablespoon olive oil
- 1 large tomato, diced
- 1 avocado
- 1/2 lime, juice
- 1 clove garlic, minced
- fresh cilantro or parsley for serving
- 1/2 can of canned beans (e.g., black or red beans), rinsed and drained

DESCRIPTION

STEP 1
Preheat the air fryer to 200°C (390°F). In a large bowl, mix the red bell pepper, green bell pepper, red onion, chili powder, salt, pepper, and olive oil.

STEP 2
Spread the vegetable mixture evenly on the tortillas and carefully transfer them to the air fryer.

STEP 3
Cook the tostadas for 8-10 minutes or until the vegetables are tender and golden brown.

STEP 4
While the tostadas are cooking, prepare the guacamole. In a bowl, mash the avocado, add lime juice, minced garlic, salt, and pepper to taste. Mix well until smooth.

STEP 5
Once the tostadas are ready, top each one with diced tomatoes, beans, and a generous amount of guacamole. Serve the hot veggie tostadas with lime wedges.

FALAFEL WITH HUMMUS

 Cooking Difficulty: 2/10

 Cooking Time: 21 minutes

 Servings: 2

INGREDIENTS

- 1 (15 oz) can chickpeas, soaked overnight and drained
- 1/2 onion, diced
- 1/4 cup parsley, chopped
- 1/4 cup cilantro, chopped
- 1 tbsp tahini
- 1 tsp ground cumin
- 1/2 tsp ground coriander
- salt and pepper to taste
- 4 pita breads
- 1/2 cup hummus

DESCRIPTION

STEP 1
Preheat Air Fryer to 400°F (200°C).

STEP 2
In a food processor, combine chickpeas, onion, parsley, cilantro, tahini, cumin, coriander, salt, and pepper. Form the mixture into falafel balls. Place falafel balls in the Air Fryer basket. Air fry for 15-20 minutes, flipping once, until falafel is golden brown.

STEP 3
Divide falafel among pita breads, top with hummus.

NUTRITIONAL INFORMATION

400 Calories, 15g Fat, 50g Carbs, 20g Protein

61

VEGAN CAULIFLOWER WINGS

 Cooking Difficulty: 1/10

 Cooking Time: 28 minutes

 Servings: 2

INGREDIENTS

- 1 head of cauliflower, cut into small florets
- 1/4 cup soy sauce
- 2 tablespoons maple syrup
- 1 tablespoon Worcestershire sauce
- 1 teaspoon smoked paprika
- 1/2 teaspoon cayenne pepper
- 1/4 cup vegetable oil

DESCRIPTION

STEP 1
Toss cauliflower florets with all ingredients in a bowl.

STEP 2
Spread cauliflower florets on a baking sheet and roast in the oven at 400°F (200°C) for 20-25 minutes or until golden brown.

NUTRITIONAL INFORMATION

195 Calories, 7g Fat, 15g Carbs, 11g Protein

VEGGIE TACOS

 Cooking Difficulty: 2/10

 Cooking Time: 12 minutes

 Servings: 4

INGREDIENTS

- 12 corn tortillas
- 1/2 cup diced red cabbage
- 1/4 cup diced red onion
- 1/4 cup diced tomatoes
- 1/4 cup canned corn
- 1/4 avocado, diced
- 1/4 cup parsley, chopped
- 1/4 cup vegan sour cream
- 1 tbsp olive oil
- 1 tsp ground cumin
- 1/2 tsp chili powder
- salt and pepper to taste

DESCRIPTION

STEP 1
Preheat Air Fryer to 400°F (200°C).

STEP 2
In a bowl, combine cabbage, onion, tomatoes, corn, avocado, vegan sour cream, olive oil, cumin, chili powder, salt, and pepper. Warm tortillas in Air Fryer for 30 seconds. Divide filling among tortillas. Fold tortillas into tacos.

STEP 3
Air fry for 2-3 minutes, or until heated through.

NUTRITIONAL INFORMATION

250 Calories, 15g Fat, 50g Carbs, 10g Protein

VEGETARIAN PIZZA

 Cooking Difficulty: 1/10   Cooking Time: 17 minutes   Servings: 2

INGREDIENTS

- 1 prepared pizza crust
- 1/4 cup tomato sauce
- 1/4 cup diced red onion
- 1/4 cup diced green olives
- 1/4 cup bell pepper
- 1/4 cup shredded vegan cheese
- 1 tbsp olive oil
- 1 tsp oregano
- basil
- salt and pepper to taste

DESCRIPTION

STEP 1
Preheat Air Fryer to 400°F (200°C).

STEP 2
Brush pizza crust with olive oil. Spread tomato sauce over crust. Top with onion, olives, bell pepper, corn, and vegan cheese. Sprinkle with oregano, salt, and pepper.

STEP 3
Air fry for 10-12 minutes, or until crust is golden brown and cheese is melted.

NUTRITIONAL INFORMATION

350 Calories, 20g Fat, 25g Carbs, 20g Protein

STUFFED GRAPE LEAVES

 Cooking Difficulty: 2/10   Cooking Time: 22 minutes   Servings: 2

INGREDIENTS

- 8 grape leaves
- 1/2 cup cooked rice
- 1/2 onion, diced
- 1/2 carrot, diced
- 1/4 cup canned corn
- 1/4 cup tomato sauce
- 1 tbsp olive oil
- 1 tsp oregano
- salt and pepper to taste

DESCRIPTION

STEP 1
Preheat Air Fryer to 400°F (200°C).

STEP 2
In a bowl, combine rice, onion, carrot, corn, tomato sauce, olive oil, oregano, salt, and pepper. Spread grape leaves on a work surface. Place a spoonful of filling on each grape leaf. Roll up the leaves to form stuffed grape leaves. Place stuffed grape leaves in the Air Fryer basket.

STEP 3
Air fry for 15-20 minutes, flipping once, until grape leaves are tender.

NUTRITIONAL INFORMATION

350 Calories, 15g Fat, 50g Carbs, 10g Protein

VEGGIE SANDWICHES

 Cooking Difficulty: 1/10

 Cooking Time: 7 minutes

 Servings: 1

INGREDIENTS

- 2 slices whole-wheat bread
- 1 tablespoons vegan cream cheese
- sliced tomatoes
- sliced avocado
- shredded romaine lettuce
- salt and pepper to taste

DESCRIPTION

STEP 1
Preheat the fryer to 400°F (200°C).

STEP 2
Spread vegan cream cheese on two slices of bread. Layer tomatoes, avocado, and romaine lettuce on one slice of bread. Top with the other slice of bread. Place sandwich in the Air Fryer basket.

STEP 3
Air fry for 3-4 minutes per side, or until bread is golden brown and cheese is melted. Serve sandwiches hot.

NUTRITIONAL INFORMATION

280 Calories, 15g Protein, 15g Fat, 25g Carbs

CAULIFLOWER STEAK

 Cooking Difficulty: 2/10   Cooking Time: 22 minutes   Servings: 2

INGREDIENTS

- 1 large head of cauliflower
- 2 tablespoons olive oil
- 1 teaspoon garlic powder
- 1/2 teaspoon paprika
- salt and pepper to taste

DESCRIPTION

STEP 1
Cut the cauliflower into 1-inch thick steaks.

STEP 2
In a small bowl, combine olive oil, garlic powder, paprika, salt, and pepper. Brush each side of the cauliflower steaks with the marinade.

STEP 3
Preheat your air fryer to 400°F (200°C). Place the cauliflower steaks in the basket in a single layer. Cook for 15-20 minutes or until golden brown, flipping halfway through.

NUTRITIONAL INFORMATION

150 Calories, 7g Fat, 10g Carbs, 5g Protein

AIR FRYER CABBAGE STEAK

 Cooking Difficulty: 1/10

 Cooking Time: 22 minutes

 Servings: 2

INGREDIENTS

- 1 young green cabbage
- 2 tablespoons olive oil
- 1 teaspoon dried garlic
- 1/2 teaspoon paprika
- salt and pepper to taste

DESCRIPTION

STEP 1
Cut the cabbage into 1-inch thick steaks. In a small bowl, combine olive oil, garlic, paprika, salt, and pepper. Brush each side of the cabbage steaks with the marinade.

STEP 2
Preheat your air fryer to 400°F (200°C). Place the cabbage steaks in the basket in a single layer. Cook for 15-20 minutes or until golden brown, flipping halfway through.

NUTRITIONAL INFORMATION

85 Calories, 4g Fat, 5g Carbs, 5g Protein

GREEN BEANS AND POTATOES

 Cooking Difficulty: 1/10

 Cooking Time: 20 minutes

 Servings: 4

INGREDIENTS

- 1 pound green beans, trimmed
- 1 pound baby potatoes, halved
- 2 tablespoons olive oil
- 1 teaspoon garlic powder
- 1/2 teaspoon paprika
- 1 teaspoon dried thyme
- 1 teaspoon dried rosemary
- 1/2 teaspoon salt
- 1/4 teaspoon black pepper
- cooking spray

DESCRIPTION

STEP 1
Preheat the air fryer to 375°F for 5 minutes. In a mixing bowl, toss the green beans and potatoes with olive oil, garlic powder, thyme, paprika rosemar ,salt, and black pepper until evenly coated.

STEP 2
Spray the air fryer basket with cooking spray. Add the green beans and potatoes to the air fryer basket in a single layer.

STEP 3
Cook for 12-15 minutes, shaking the basket every 5 minutes until the green beans and potatoes are tender and lightly browned. Serve.

NUTRITIONAL INFORMATION

Calories 212, Fat 5g, Carbs 34g, Protein 5g

AIR FRYER SWEET POTATO AND KALE

| Cooking Difficulty: 2/10 | Cooking Time: 15 minutes | Servings: 2 |

NUTRITIONAL INFORMATION

Calories 310, Fat 10g, Carbs 17g, Protein 9g

INGREDIENTS

- 2 medium sweet potatoes, cut into cubes
- 1 bunch of kale, chopped
- 2 tablespoons olive oil
- 1 teaspoon garlic powder
- 1/2 teaspoon turmeric
- salt and pepper to taste

DESCRIPTION

STEP 1
Preheat your oven to 400°F (200°C). Toss the sweet potato cubes with olive oil, garlic powder, turmeric, salt, and pepper on a baking sheet.

STEP 2
Roast the sweet potatoes in the oven for 20-25 minutes, or until tender and slightly browned.

STEP 3
While the sweet potatoes are roasting, preheat your air fryer to 400°F (200°C). Toss the chopped kale with olive oil, salt, and pepper.

STEP 4
Cook the kale in the air fryer for 5-7 minutes, or until crispy.

STEP 5
Remove the roasted sweet potatoes from the oven and the crispy kale from the air fryer. Combine in a bowl.

SPICED CHICKPEAS

 Cooking Difficulty: 1/10   Cooking Time: 24 minutes   Servings: 2

INGREDIENTS

- 1 can of chickpeas, rinsed and drained
- 2 tablespoons olive oil
- 1 teaspoon paprika
- 1/2 teaspoon ground coriander
- 1/4 teaspoon cayenne pepper (adjust to taste)
- 1/2 teaspoon salt
- 1/4 teaspoon black pepper

DESCRIPTION

STEP 1
In a small bowl, mix together the olive oil, paprika, coriander, cayenne pepper, salt, and black pepper. Add the chickpeas to the bowl and toss to coat evenly.

STEP 2
Preheat your air fryer to 400°F (200°C). Add the chickpeas to the basket in a single layer and cook for 15-20 minutes, shaking the basket halfway through, until crispy and golden brown.

STEP 3
Enjoy as a snack or add to your favorite salads.

NUTRITIONAL INFORMATION

210 Calories, 12g Protein, 7g Fat, 15g Carbs

AIR FRYER YOUNG CARROTS

 Cooking Difficulty: 1/10　 Cooking Time: 18 minutes　 Servings: 4

INGREDIENTS

- 1 pound young carrots, scrubbed
- 1 tablespoon olive oil
- 1/2 teaspoon garlic powder
- 1/4 teaspoon onion powder
- 1/4 teaspoon dried thyme
- salt and pepper to taste

DESCRIPTION

STEP 1
Preheat your air fryer to 400°F (200°C). Scrub the young carrots and trim off any tough ends..

STEP 2
In a bowl, combine the olive oil, garlic powder, onion powder, dried thyme, salt, and pepper. Toss the carrots in the seasoning mixture until they are evenly coated.

STEP 3
Place the seasoned carrots in the air fryer basket in a single layer. Cook for 10-15 minutes, or until the carrots are tender and slightly browned, shaking the basket halfway through.

NUTRITIONAL INFORMATION

205 Calories, 9g Fat, 11g Carbs, 15g Protein

CHICKPEA, SPINACH, AND KALE PATTIES

 Cooking Difficulty: 1/10
 Cooking Time: 24 minutes
 Servings: 2

INGREDIENTS

- 1 can chickpeas (15 oz), rinsed and drained
- 1 bunch spinach
- 1 kale leaf
- 1 onion
- 2 cloves garlic
- 1/4 cup breadcrumbs
- 1 tbsp ground cumin
- 1/2 tsp ground coriander
- salt, pepper to taste
- olive oil

DESCRIPTION

STEP 1
Chop all ingredients except oil, combine in a bowl. Form into patties.

STEP 2
Grease air fryer basket with oil. Cook patties at 200°C for 15-18 minutes, flipping halfway through.

NUTRITIONAL INFORMATION

340 Calories, 38g Protein, 10g Fat, 35g Carbs

AIR FRYER ROASTED VEGETABLES

 Cooking Difficulty: 2/10

 Cooking Time: 25 minutes

 Servings: 4

NUTRITIONAL INFORMATION

110 Calories, 4g Protein, 3g Fat, 5g Carbs

INGREDIENTS

- 1 pound mushrooms (such as button or shiitake), sliced
- 1 red onion, sliced
- 1 bell pepper, sliced
- 1 zucchini, diced
- 2 tablespoons olive oil
- 1 clove garlic, minced
- salt and pepper to taste
- fresh herbs (such as rosemary, thyme, or oregano) to taste

DESCRIPTION

STEP 1
Slice the mushrooms, onion, bell pepper, and zucchini into bite-sized pieces.

STEP 2
In a large bowl, combine the olive oil, minced garlic, salt, pepper, and your choice of fresh herbs. Add the prepared vegetables and toss to coat evenly.

STEP 3
Place half of the vegetables in the air fryer basket in a single layer.

STEP 4
Set the air fryer to 400°F (200°C) and cook for 10-12 minutes.

STEP 5
Remove the basket and carefully turn the vegetables. Add the remaining vegetables and return to the air fryer.

STEP 6
Cook for an additional 8-10 minutes, or until the vegetables are tender and golden brown. Shake the basket halfway through cooking for even browning.

SPICEY CARROTS

 Cooking Difficulty: 1/10   Cooking Time: 24 minutes   Servings: 2

INGREDIENTS

- 4 medium carrots
- 1 tablespoon olive oil
- 1/2 teaspoon ground turmeric
- 1/4 teaspoon ground coriander
- 1/4 teaspoon ground ginger
- 1/4 teaspoon cayenne pepper (adjust to taste)
- salt and black pepper to taste
- fresh herbs (cilantro, parsley) for serving

DESCRIPTION

STEP 1
Preheat your Air Fryer to 400°F (200°C). Wash the carrots thoroughly and cut them into 1/4-inch thick medallions.

STEP 2
In a large bowl, toss the carrots with olive oil, turmeric, coriander, ginger, cayenne pepper, salt, and black pepper. Mix until the carrots are evenly coated.

STEP 3
Place the carrots in a single layer in the Air Fryer basket. Cook for 15-20 minutes or until tender and golden brown, shaking the basket halfway through.

NUTRITIONAL INFORMATION

198 Calories, 10g Fat, 14g Carbs, 12g Protein

ROASTED ARTICHOKE HEARTS

 Cooking Difficulty: 2/10

 Cooking Time: 28 minutes

 Servings: 2

INGREDIENTS

- 2 large artichokes
- 1/4 cup olive oil
- 2 cloves garlic, minced
- 1 tablespoon lemon juice
- 1 teaspoon dried oregano
- 1/2 teaspoon red pepper flakes
- salt and black pepper to taste

DESCRIPTION

STEP 1
Cut the artichokes in half lengthwise. Use a spoon to scoop out the fuzzy choke and tough inner leaves.

STEP 2
In a small bowl, whisk together olive oil, minced garlic, lemon juice, oregano, red pepper flakes, salt, and pepper.

STEP 3
Brush the cut sides of the artichoke hearts generously with the marinade. Place the artichoke halves, cut side down, in the Air Fryer basket. Cook at 380°F (190°C) for 20-25 minutes, or until tender and the leaves pull away easily.

NUTRITIONAL INFORMATION

285 Calories, 18g Protein, 9g Fat, 15g Carbs

RED AND YELLOW BELL PEPPERS

 Cooking Difficulty: 1/10
 Cooking Time: 12 minutes
 Servings: 4

INGREDIENTS

- 2 red bell peppers, sliced
- 2 yellow bell peppers, sliced
- 1 tablespoon olive oil
- 1 teaspoon garlic powder
- salt
- black pepper
- cooking spray
- fresh cilantro for garnish

DESCRIPTION

STEP 1
Preheat the air fryer to 375°F for 5 minutes. In a mixing bowl, toss the sliced red and yellow bell peppers with the olive oil, garlic powder, salt, and black pepper until evenly coated.

STEP 2
Spray the air fryer basket with cooking spray. Add the sliced bell peppers to the air fryer basket in a single layer.

STEP 3
Cook for 8-10 minutes, shaking the basket every 3-4 minutes until the bell peppers are tender and lightly charred. Serve.

NUTRITIONAL INFORMATION

Calories 72, Fat 4g, Carbs 9g, Protein 2g

VEGETARIAN BURRITO

 Cooking Difficulty: 2/10　　 Cooking Time: 10 minutes　　 Servings: 4

INGREDIENTS

- 4 whole wheat tortillas
- 1 cup cooked brown rice
- 1 can (400g) black beans, drained and rinsed
- 1 cup corn, fresh or frozen
- 1 large tomato, diced
- 1 cup shredded red cabbage
- juice of 1 lime
- fresh cilantro for garnish
- salt and pepper to taste

DESCRIPTION

STEP 1
In a bowl, mix cooked brown rice, black beans, corn, and tomatoes.

STEP 2
Begin assembling the burrito on a tortilla, adding the rice and bean mixture, and red cabbage. Drizzle lime juice and sprinkle fresh cilantro.

STEP 3
Roll up the burrito and place it in the Air Fryer. Start the Air Fryer for 5-7 minutes at 180°C.

NUTRITIONAL INFORMATION

290 Calories, 9g Protein, 11g Fat, 7,4g Carbs

BRUSSELS SPROUTS WITH POMEGRANATE SEEDS

 Cooking Difficulty: 2/10

 Cooking Time: 24 minutes

 Servings: 2

INGREDIENTS

- 1 pound brussels sprouts, halved
- 1 tablespoon olive oil
- 1/4 teaspoon garlic powder
- 1/4 teaspoon onion powder
- 1/4 teaspoon smoked paprika
- salt and black pepper to taste
- 1/4 cup pomegranate seeds

DESCRIPTION

STEP 1
Preheat your Air Fryer to 400°F (200°C). Cut the Brussels sprouts in half and toss them in a bowl with olive oil, garlic powder, onion powder, smoked paprika, salt, and pepper.

STEP 2
Place the Brussels sprouts in a single layer in the Air Fryer basket. Cook for 18-22 minutes, or until tender and slightly browned, shaking the basket halfway through. Toss the cooked Brussels sprouts with pomegranate seeds. Serve immediately.

NUTRITIONAL INFORMATION

Calories 272, Fat 4g, Carbs 9g, Protein 7g

SWEET CHILI TOFU BITES

 Cooking Difficulty: 3/10   Cooking Time: 25 minutes   Servings: 2

INGREDIENTS

- 12 ounces extra-firm tofu, cubed
- 2 tablespoons soy sauce
- 2 tablespoons date syrup
- 1 tablespoon rice vinegar
- 1 teaspoon sesame oil
- 1/2 teaspoon red pepper flakes
- 1/4 teaspoon ground ginger
- 1 clove garlic, minced
- 1 green onion, thinly sliced
- 1 tablespoon sesame seeds

DESCRIPTION

STEP 1
Preheat your Air Fryer to 400°F (200°C). Gently press the tofu between paper towels to remove excess moisture.

STEP 2
In a small bowl, whisk together soy sauce, date syrup, rice vinegar, sesame oil, red pepper flakes, ginger, and garlic.

STEP 3
Place the tofu cubes in the Air Fryer basket and drizzle with the sauce. Toss to coat. Cook for 15-20 minutes, shaking the basket halfway through. Transfer the tofu to a serving plate and sprinkle with green onions and sesame seeds.

NUTRITIONAL INFORMATION

Calories 220, Fat 12g, Carbs 14g, Protein 16g

BRUSSELS SPROUTS WITH MUSHROOMS

 Cooking Difficulty: 2/10

 Cooking Time: 25 minutes

 Servings: 2

INGREDIENTS

- 1 cup brussels sprouts, halved
- 1 cup mushrooms, halved
- 2 tablespoons olive oil
- 2 cloves garlic, minced
- salt and pepper to taste
- fresh herbs (parsley, thyme, or rosemary), chopped

DESCRIPTION

STEP 1
Preheat your air fryer to 180°C (360°F). In a large bowl, toss Brussels sprouts, mushrooms, olive oil, and minced garlic until evenly coated.

STEP 2
Spread the vegetables evenly on the air fryer tray in a single layer. Season with salt and pepper. Air fry for 15-20 minutes until Brussels sprouts are golden and tender, and mushrooms are cooked through. Stir the vegetables occasionally for even cooking. Once done, sprinkle with fresh herbs before serving.

NUTRITIONAL INFORMATION

Calories 120, Fat 8g, Carbs 9g, Protein 4g

SNACKS & DESSERTS

SPICY CORN

 Cooking Difficulty: 2/10   Cooking Time: 18 minutes   Servings: 2

INGREDIENTS

- 2 ears of corn, husks removed
- 2 tablespoons vegan butter
- 1 teaspoon chili powder
- 1/2 teaspoon garlic powder
- 1/4 teaspoon onion powder
- 1/4 teaspoon smoked paprika
- 1/8 teaspoon cayenne pepper (adjust to taste)
- salt and black pepper to taste
- fresh cilantro, for serving (optional)
- lime wedges, for serving (optional)

DESCRIPTION

STEP 1
Preheat your Air Fryer to 400°F (200°C). Brush the corn cobs with vegan butter. In a small bowl, combine chili powder, garlic powder, onion powder, smoked paprika, cayenne pepper, salt, and black pepper. Sprinkle the seasoning mixture evenly over the corn cobs, making sure to coat all sides.

STEP 2
Place the corn cobs in the Air Fryer basket. Cook for 10-15 minutes, or until the corn is tender and slightly charred, flipping halfway through. Remove the corn from the Air Fryer and serve immediately.

NUTRITIONAL INFORMATION

190 Calories, 11g Protein, 7g Fat, 7,4g Carbs

ALMOND-CRUSTED AIR FRYER GREEN BEANS

 Cooking Difficulty: 2/10
 Cooking Time: 15 minutes
 Servings: 2

NUTRITIONAL INFORMATION

120 Calories, 9g Protein, 5g Fat, 10g Carbs

INGREDIENTS

- 1 pound green beans, trimmed
- 1/4 cup almond flour
- 1 tablespoon olive oil
- 1/4 teaspoon garlic powder
- 1/4 teaspoon onion powder
- 1/8 teaspoon cayenne pepper (adjust to taste)
- salt and black pepper to taste
- 1 tablespoon vegan butter

DESCRIPTION

STEP 1
Preheat your Air Fryer to 400°F (200°C).

STEP 2
In a shallow bowl, combine almond flour, olive oil, garlic powder, onion powder, cayenne pepper, salt, and black pepper.

STEP 3
Toss the green beans in the almond flour mixture until evenly coated.

STEP 4
Place the coated green beans in the Air Fryer basket in a single layer. Cook for 8-10 minutes, shaking the basket halfway through, until the green beans are tender-crisp and the almond coating is golden brown.

STEP 5
Drizzle the cooked green beans with vagan butter.

STEP 6
Serve immediately.

VEGAN CAULIFLOWER

 Cooking Difficulty: 1/10    Cooking Time: 40 minutes   Servings: 4

INGREDIENTS

- 1 large head of cauliflower
- 1/4 cup gluten-free breadcrumbs (or crushed nuts)
- 2 tablespoons vegetable oil (olive, avocado, or coconut)
- 1 teaspoon smoked paprika
- 1/2 teaspoon garlic powder
- 1/4 teaspoon cayenne pepper (adjust to taste)
- 1/4 cup chopped fresh parsley
- salt and pepper to taste

DESCRIPTION

STEP 1
Preheat your air fryer to 400°F (200°C). Trim the cauliflower, leaving the stem intact to hold it together. Rinse well and pat dry. In a small bowl, combine the breadcrumbs, oil, smoked paprika, garlic powder, cayenne pepper, parsley, salt, and pepper.

STEP 2
Brush the cauliflower with vegetable oil and then coat it evenly with the breadcrumb mixture. Place the cauliflower in the air fryer basket, stem-side down. Cook for 30-35 minutes, or until the cauliflower is tender and the crust is golden brown.

NUTRITIONAL INFORMATION
298 Calories, 11g Fat, 4g Carbs, 12g Protein

SPICED AIR FRYER NUTS

 Cooking Difficulty: 1/10

 Cooking Time: 12 minutes

 Servings: 4

INGREDIENTS

- 1 cup mixed nuts (such as almonds, cashews, and pecans)
- 1 tablespoon olive oil
- 1 teaspoon smoked paprika
- 1/2 teaspoon garlic powder
- 1/4 teaspoon cayenne pepper
- 1/4 teaspoon ground cumin
- 1/4 teaspoon sea salt

DESCRIPTION

STEP 1
Preheat air fryer to 160°C (320°F). Toss nuts with oil until coated. Combine spices in a bowl. Sprinkle spice mix over nuts, toss to coat.

STEP 2
Coat air fryer basket with cooking spray. Spread nuts in a single layer in basket. Air fry for 8-10 minutes, shaking halfway. Watch carefully to prevent burning. Cool before serving.

NUTRITIONAL INFORMATION

Calories: 220, Fat: 19g, Carbs:g, Protein: 6g

SPICED APPLE WEDGES WITH CHIA PUDDING

 Cooking Difficulty: 2/10

 Cooking Time: 25 minutes

 Servings: 2

NUTRITIONAL INFORMATION

380 Calories, 17g Protein, 8g Fat, 25g Carbs

INGREDIENTS

for the apples:
- 2 large apples, cut in half and cored
- 1 tablespoon vegan butter
- 1/2 teaspoon cinnamon
- 1/4 teaspoon nutmeg
- 1/4 teaspoon ground cloves
- pinch of salt
- sugar to taste (optional)

for the chia pudding:
- 1/4 cup chia seeds
- 1 cup milk (coconut, or almond)
- 1 tablespoon honey or maple syrup
- vanilla extract to taste

DESCRIPTION

STEP 1
Preheat your Air Fryer to 400°F (200°C).

STEP 2
In a small bowl, combine the butter, cinnamon, nutmeg, cloves, salt, and sugar (if using). Rub this mixture into the cut sides of the apples.

STEP 3
Place the apple halves, cut-side down, in the Air Fryer basket. Cook for 15-20 minutes, or until tender.

STEP 4
In a glass jar or bowl, whisk together the chia seeds, milk, maple syrup, and vanilla. Cover and refrigerate for at least 2 hours, or overnight, until the chia seeds have absorbed the liquid and the pudding has thickened.

STEP 5
Serve the warm, spiced apple halves with a side of chia pudding.

SPICY CARAMELIZED BANANAS

 Cooking Difficulty: 1/10

 Cooking Time: 10 minutes

 Servings: 4

INGREDIENTS

- 2 ripe bananas, sliced
- 2 tablespoons maple syrup
- 1 teaspoon coconut oil
- 1/4 teaspoon ground cinnamon
- 1/4 teaspoon ground ginger
- pinch of cayenne pepper
- pinch of sea salt

DESCRIPTION

STEP 1
Preheat your Air Fryer to 400°F (200°C). In a bowl, toss the banana slices with maple syrup, coconut oil, cinnamon, ginger, cayenne pepper, and sea salt.

STEP 2
Place the banana slices in a single layer in the Air Fryer basket. Cook for 5-7 minutes, or until the bananas are caramelized and slightly crispy. Serve the caramelized bananas warm as a dessert or a healthy snack.

NUTRITIONAL INFORMATION
400 Calories, 18g Fat, 28g Carbs, 22g Protein

ROASTED QUINCE STUFFED WITH NUTS

 Cooking Difficulty: 2/10  Cooking Time: 25 minutes Servings: 2

INGREDIENTS

- 2 quinces
- 1/4 cup chopped walnuts
- 1 tablespoon honey
- 1 teaspoon cinnamon
- pinch of nutmeg
- juice of half a lemon

DESCRIPTION

STEP 1
Preheat your air fryer to 400°F (200°C). Cut the quince in half and carefully remove the core, creating a small cavity.

STEP 2
Mix the chopped walnuts, honey, cinnamon, nutmeg, and lemon juice. Fill each half of the quince with the nut mixture.

STEP 3
Place the quince halves in the air fryer basket, cut side down. Cook for 15-20 minutes or until the quince is soft and golden brown. Serve warm.

NUTRITIONAL INFORMATION

Calories 270, Fat 8g, Carbs 17g, Protein 16g

SWEET POTATO CHIPS

 Cooking Difficulty: 1/10 Cooking Time: 20 minutes Servings: 4

INGREDIENTS

- 2 sweet potato
- 1 tbsp olive oil or coconut oil
- 1/2 tsp brown sugar (optional)
- 1/2 tsp ground coriander
- 1/4 tsp turmeric
- salt and pepper to taste

DESCRIPTION

STEP 1
Preheat the air fryer to 190°C (375°F). Wash the sweet potato thoroughly and pat it dry. Slice the sweet potato into thin slices or rings. In a large bowl, mix the olive oil, brown sugar (if using), ground coriander, turmeric, salt, and pepper. Add the sliced sweet potato to the bowl and toss until evenly coated with the oil mixture.

STEP 2
Arrange the sweet potato in a single layer in the air fryer basket. Air fry the sweet potato for 12-15 minutes, flipping occasionally for even cooking. Carefully remove the cooked chips from the air fryer and let them cool slightly before serving.

NUTRITIONAL INFORMATION

120 Calories, 3g Fat, 22g Carbs, 2g Protein

CARROT CHIPS

 Cooking Difficulty: 1/10

 Cooking Time: 17 minutes

 Servings: 4

INGREDIENTS

- 4 medium carrots
- 1 tablespoon olive oil
- salt and pepper to taste
- any other spices (such as paprika, garlic powder) optional

DESCRIPTION

STEP 1
Preheat the air fryer to 180°C (350°F). Wash and dry 2 medium carrots, then slice them thinly. Toss the carrot slices with 1 tablespoon of olive oil, salt, and pepper.

STEP 2
Arrange the carrot slices in a single layer in the air fryer basket. Air fry at 180°C (350°F) for 10-15 minutes until golden brown and crispy. Check occasionally and toss if needed for even cooking.

NUTRITIONAL INFORMATION

Calories 50, Fat 3g, Carbs 5g, Protein 1g

BEET CHIPS

 Cooking Difficulty: 2/10
 Cooking Time: 25 minutes
 Servings: 3

NUTRITIONAL INFORMATION

Calories 80, Fat 4g, Carbs 7g, Protein 1g

INGREDIENTS

- 3 medium beets
- 1 tablespoon olive oil
- salt
- pepper
- fresh herbs for garnish

DESCRIPTION

STEP 1
Preheat the air fryer to 180°C (350°F).

STEP 2
On a cutting board, slice the beets into thin slices about 1 millimeter thick.

STEP 3
In a large bowl, toss the sliced beets with olive oil until evenly coated. Season the beets with salt and pepper to taste.

STEP 4
Arrange the beet slices in a single layer in the air fryer basket, ensuring they are not overcrowded.

STEP 5
Air fry the beet chips for 15-20 minutes, flipping halfway through, until they are crispy and golden brown.

STEP 6
Once cooked, remove the beet chips from the air fryer and transfer them to a paper towel to remove any excess oil. Serve the hot beet chips, garnished with fresh herbs if desired.

CONCLUSION

Congratulations! You've completed «Plant-Based Air Fryer Cookbook,» and now you have a wealth of tools and recipes to bring healthy and delicious eating into your life. I hope this book has inspired you to embark on culinary adventures and has made adhering to a plant-based diet both easy and enjoyable. Using an air fryer to prepare meals is not only convenient and quick but also helps preserve the nutritional value of your ingredients while giving them a crispy texture and rich flavor. From delectable breakfasts and light lunches to hearty dinners and sweet treats, this book offers recipes to satisfy even the most discerning palate.

Remember, transitioning to a plant-based diet is a journey, not a destination. Don't be afraid to experiment with new ingredients and cooking techniques. Each recipe in this book can be tailored to suit your tastes and preferences. The key is to enjoy the process and embrace each new discovery in your kitchen.

Thank you for choosing «Plant-Based Air Fryer Cookbook.» May every culinary experience be filled with joy and satisfaction, and may your meals always be both tasty and nutritious. Health and well-being are not just goals but a way of life. May your cooking journey bring you pleasure and good health!

Alan Caplan

Printed in Great Britain
by Amazon